T0115032

ILORIN Ó
Poetry of Praise

ILORIN Ó
Poetry of Praise

By

Abdul-Rasheed Na'Allah

malthouse

Malthouse Press Limited

Lagos, Benin, Ibadan, Jos, Port-Harcourt, Zaria

© Abdul-Rasheed Na'Allah 2018
First Published 2018
ISBN: 978-978-55798-6-4

Published and manufactured in Nigeria by

Malthouse Press Limited
43 Onitana Street, Off Stadium Hotel Road,
Off Western Avenue, Lagos Mainland
E-mail: malthouselagos@gmail.com
malthouse_press@yahoo.com
Tel: +234 802 600 3203

Distributors:
African Books Collective Ltd
Email: abc@africanbookscollective.com
Website: http://www.africanbookscollective.com

Dedication

For

My Darling Karamah, Ramata Elebolo Ayinke Ese, Omo Ahmad
Kamal Khalifa Adabiyya, Omo-omo Muhammadu Kamaludeen
Al-Adab, Omo Iya Niyi, Omo Ilorin!

Acknowledgements

I owe a great deal of gratitude to many people for the assistance I got in putting this volume together: my family, first and foremost, nuclear and extended family, then my friends and academic colleagues. Erica (Potterbaum) Reckamp, for editing and critical comments. My Personal Asssistant, AbdulRafiu Gold, for running errands for me whenever I need something urgent. More importantly, I acknowledge the love, care and prayers of all Ilorin people, wherever I meet them in and out of the community I am always overwhelmed by their sincere prayers and love. I also acknowledge my parents who ensured that I received a true cultural education about my people and community. With all this help, writing this poetry has been a wonderful experience.

The Poems

Section I

Amalgamation
Greatness in the home of Jurists!
Ukku Ukku de o!
Ibrahim Kaula Niyas *wa si'lorin!*
Garin Ilori, Garin aduha!
'Dan Mutunci, 'Dan Ilori
Ilorin ó!
Onikepe Aduke Opo

Section 2

Baban Gani Eto!
Shehu Salihu Baba Oba
AbdulKadir *Orire*
Ibrahim Sulu Gambari, Emir of Dignity
Kayo-Kayo
The First Makama of Ilorin
Sherifu-deen of Ilorin
Oniwasi Agbaye, Aminullahi!

Section 3

En so nilorin o eheee!
Khalifatu Adabiyya, *Alabi Ese!*
Nda Salati

Alfa Belgore
Ibrahim, the Lion of Love
Kosibi Tolohun *o si, ama Ilorin ninsun*
Ilorin Ete!

Section 4

Saka Nuru
Omo Ilorin
Loya AbdulRazak, *Omo Ukku Ukku!*
Wazirin Geri, the test of a patriot!
Pacesetters
Bukola hasn't risen yet!
The Corners of Ilorin

Section 5

Aso-Ofi, clothes of all ages!
Warankasi
Why the Sun has Not Diminished in Sunlight
Alfa Na'Allah
Bilikisu *Esuu Oke*
Ore kii y'ore!
Tuworesi
Abebi Akosile

Introduction

Ilorin Ó is the second volume in the Ilorin trilogy, and it continues the praise poetry of my City of Birth, Ilorin, the enigmatic city of our time. The multicultural nature of Ilorin is reflected in the poems, and so is its Islamic status. The indigenes of Ilorin have long claimed that it doesn't matter to them if a person insults an ethnic identity—they have no passion for ethnicity: Yoruba, Hausa, Fulani, Baruba, Nupe, Kamberi. As long as someone does not insult another's faith, there is no problem with an Ilorin person. Faith is a common source of unity to the people and it almost entirely eliminates ethnic rivalry in Ilorin. Faith is the thread that brings all Ilorin people together, and to which they now have "allegiance and emotional attachment" (a yardstick once used by Oladele Awobuluyi to denote people's feelings towards their indigenous languages). In Ilorin's case, a predominantly Moslem city, Islam has brought tremendous spiritual growth and blessings.

So what typical indigenous people may have towards their ethnic language is what Ilorin has towards religion. Ilorin therefore counters Awobuluyi in this instance. A popular phrase in the praise poetry of Ilorin among the Yoruba is *Ilu tobi to yi ò leegun*, "a city as big as this has no masquerade," expressing the Yoruba paradox that a very big town such as Ilorin has no Egungun. This is further evidence that the Yoruba world has turned away from a single government/culture as leader and rather turned towards religious leaders.

This volume represents all facets of praise poetry as a demonstration of passion and love, at times even a critical appraisal of an item of praise. What I have done here is express an overriding craving for my city and its people, and I reflected passionately on my personal experience of being a child of Ilorin. The poems, as usual, are in three languages: Hausa, Yoruba and English, with Yoruba and English poems a bit more predominant in this volume.

The poetry seeks to rekindle in an Ilorin person a sense of history and a sense of cultural pride, and for a non-Ilorin provide some insight into what it means to have an Ilorin identity. It can be difficult to separate the use of the word "Ilorin" from meaning a city to meaning a person, an indigene, or even to meaning the form of Yoruba language spoken in Ilorin. *So Ilorin si mi*, "Speak Ilorin to me," is often what you hear whenever patriotism takes over an elder scolding the younger Ilorin person speaking the English language.

The word, "Ilorin," as used among Ilorin people also means the philosophy, the attitude, the characteristics, the actions and the inactions, as well as the semantics of actions and inactions of Ilorin persons. There is a saying among Ilorin people, *ti eyan ba kewu, oni lati ke Ilorin kun*, "a person who learns the Quran must also have to learn Ilorin with it." Interestingly, this also means that if you pride yourself in acquiring western education without "learning Ilorin," western education alone may not confer much effectiveness on you in the community! Your actions could simply portray you as an *ágò*, "one without learning," *alaigbon*, "one without wisdom/cleverness /smartness," within the community no matter how learned you are in western content.

It would be correct to say that Yoruba poems in this volume are written in Ilorin Yoruba, and therefore convey the flavour of the Ilorin local language. I am convinced as I try to express in many forums that a literary work has to carry the original dialect of the author to ring true and no effort must be made to force such work to conform to any so-called standard form of the language in which an author has given birth to or created a work.

Section 1

Amalgamation

Unification
Multiples unified!
Merger
Diversities merged!
Interaction
Differences interacted
Consolidation
Scatterings consolidated
Integration
Pluralities integrated!
The House of plurality
The City of Multiples
The Town of Diversity
The Dwelling of Differences
The Domicile of those previously scattered in clans
Now ruled from the central lineage:
Alimi Central
Shehu Central
Alfa Alimi Central
Shehu Alimi Central
No better amalgamates anywhere
Than these Ilorinians unified in plurality
Ilorin of cultural diversity
Ethnicities fused!
Together in faith!

Greatness in the home of Jurists!

What other city can boast
Of this height in the eyes of jurists
This rate at which its own become legends of law
Ilorin the City of Law!
Only Ilorin, legal aramanda of Justice
Ilorin, legal in terms of fairness and bravery
The Ilorin jurists are jurists for humaneness:
Ancestral lineage, Ilorin lineage of humaneness!
Aliyu AbdulKadir, Legend of fairness
The Emir who held the sword in honour of the downtrodden
Overruled the powerful to take cues from the poor
That power is held in trust for Allah
Ilorin is the City where all go to visit the legends of Laws
From the ages of fearless Lions, the Amirs of the Believers
To the ages of military and political rulers, when the
    straightness of lines
Bent by the furnace of fire!
Ilorin's jurists—leading from the Court of Appeals to the
    Supreme Court
Ushered the judgments according to their heredity
Legends in Fairness, Lions in Bravery!
No other town
Boasts of this history of dual Audacity
Our legends of the Bench, Ilorin is forever proud!
Alfa Belgore of Ilorin
Mustapha Akanbi of Ilorin!
Duality Bravery, Duality Courage,
Ilorin ni! Wallahi Ilorin ni!

Ukku Ukku de o!

Ukku Ukku de o
Gambari de o
Gambari loko awa o!
Gambari loko awa o!

Ilorin de bintin de
Gambari de bintin de
Arogun masa de bintin de
Baruba de bintin de
Ajasa de bintin de
Alohunmata de bintin de
Jabata de bintin de
Olohungbebe de bintin de
Fulani de bintin de
Omoadua de bintin de
Ilorin de bintin de
Alalubose de bintin de
Kasandubu de bintin de
Okutagidi de bintin de
Ilorin de bintin de
Oni tanganran de bintin de
Alanamu de bintin de
Apaokagi de bintin de
Ilorin de bintin de
Babamasa de bintin de
Oniguguru de bintin de
Onikijipa de bintin de

Kuranga de bintin de
Ajikobi de bintin de
Aare de bintin de
Akodudu de bintin de
Itaajia de bintin de
Odekobi de bintin de
Korotapa de bintin de
Ubandawaki de bintinde
Oniwiridi de bintin de
Gobiri de bintin de
Ilorin de bintin de
Afa alimi de bintin de

Omo Ilorin loko awa o!
Akewusola loko awa o!
Gambari loko awa o!
Ukku ukku loko awa o!

Ibrahim Kaula Niyas *wa si'lorin!*

Ilorin ilu woli
Ilu aafa
Ilu ti Ibrahim Kaula Niyas fi sogangan okan to
To fi rii ni Ilu alfaari
Taaba ko egbawa ilu jo
Teeni ni ki Omo Kaula omu kan soso
Ife awon iye woli olohun to fi Ilorin sele
Ife Shehu Alimi tofi Ilorin selu
Ife Olohun gan, to sa ilu Ilorin lesa
Oti to fun Kaula ko wo lorin
Ten ba ma pe Kaula nife Ilorin
Se bi ema wipe nitori alubarika tolohun fun lorun ni
Ojulowo Omo kaula o ni yapa
Lati wa tele Ibrahim Niyas ninu ife toni si ilu alaafia
Ilu nio! Ilu islamu ni, Ilu ope, ilu aduha
Ilu Ilorin, tojepe gbogbo ijo islamu yan layo
Bo domoda, bo de Gambari abi ode Oriokoo
Awon omo Kaula nse ope folohun Oba
Wipe Eni tobati ri won ni Ilorin Ilu aafa
Mapee Ibrahim kaula Niyas! wa nibe!

Garin Ilori, Garin aduha!

Nasan kasan Allah shi yace akira shi, kuma shi zai amza
Haka dai ake cewa aduahu ce takobin musulumi
Watau a garin Ilorin ake gan takobin
In kana son kaga inda rana da dare, yamma da marece,
Da antashi tseye, da ruguma ko ana kwance,
Inda yo yaya ake ana wanka cikin kungi aduha
Sai kaje Ilorin, Garin Alimi
A Ilori ne ake da hakimi wai shi Hakimin aduha
A garin da dare da rana, kulla yaomi, akwai aduhan sa'a,
Anan Ilori, aduha fa abinci ne, ita ce iska da ake sha, it ce
     fura it ace nono
 Aduha ce tuwo aduha ce miyan, ita kuma ce nama masoyin
     kubewa
Gidan Ilorin Gidan Sarkin aduha
In za'a kyauta zaayi kirari ta gari,
Kirarin Sarkin Musulumi, sai ace Sarkin Aduha!
Anan gidan Alimi, sauren aduha,
Saukakken Kurani sau ba iyaka ko da yaushe
Rokon Ilori rokon albarka
Allah ya Allah Ya Allahu, kai kabba yaran Ilori aduha
     Kurani
Kai kabbasu Fatiha ta albarka,
Ya Allah ya Allahu Ya Allah
Madaukakin Sarki,
Ka kara wa albarka duk aihuwan Ilori mai aduha!

'Dan Mutunci, 'Dan Ilori

'Dan Ilori akwai mutunci
'Dan Ilori ana Fulani
Ko ina ka ga wani yana kunya, d'an Ilori kenan mai
    mutunci

Watau wata rana na dawo gida daga aiki
Sai na angi wani wai shi Babban Malami
Da tasbia da kur'an ga hannu
Bakin sa sai rawa yana zufa da karatu
Sai na ce masa, haba wannan malami
Ba karatu kake ba, wayace sai kayi gumi kafin Allah yaji
Yace kai ina kunnen ka, ai wanna dunmi nawa, don
    girmama Ubangidi ne, watau shi yayi murya na
Lalle, ban gane ba, wannan d'an taliki malami, yana
    laagun yana karatu alkur'an
Yace don Allah ne
Wanna lawani daka tab'a samma, shin saikasa haka kafin
    Allah yaji?
Malami bai hamza ba, sai kasa yake duba
Kai Malami da kai nake, shin wayace sai da rawani mai
    dogon hannu zuwa sama
Ka gan ya gyale ni, agidan Ilori, iriiri,
Malamai iri-iri, wasu da gaimu tab'a k'asa, wasu da
    rawani tab'a sama
Duk dan adini, wai sunna sukai
Ya Allah, ya Allah ina aduha
Wannan gari da iyan sunna

Wannan k'asan da iya mutunci
Kabasu duk abunda mutuci kai sayuwa
Kabasu alheri na masun kunya
Ka karba aduhan su, su sama nag aba dukkan dan uwan
    sun a gari
Wannan Mutane, d'an muttunci d'an Ilori!

Ilorin Ó!

Ilu Alafia ile ayo ilu aponle
Ilorin ilu alfari, ilu al-kalami
Ilu ti wonti fi kalamu se faari
Ilu ti won fi wala dara ninu ima
Ilu ima-ijinle, ilu owo, ilu faaji
Ilu ifayabale, Ilorin nin jebe lawujo
Ilorin ó, ilu AbdulSalami, Ilu AbdulKadiri
Ilu Sulu Aiyelabowo
Ilu Shehu Ibrahima Oba Ilorin
Ilorin ó
Gbogbo ara, alejo towa si Ilorin
Eyi tenbanfe ni e so
Eso nkan tayayin nla kaka si
Ilorin lede, ef'edo lori oronro
Ilu ifaya bale lede, efi okan bale s'odo Olohun
Kosibi t'olohun osi, Ama Ilorin nin sun!

Onikepe Aduke Opo

The lion has a daughter, her name is lioness!
He has a baby that all come around to pamper.
Onikepe, all who care for her come together!
A baby that all love, and has the gene of loving
Aduke Opo, daughter of Ilorin, granddaughter of the sages of
     the city
It is from the womb that a baby hears the recitation of the
     Quran
She hears the sound of reading from her parents before she
     learns to talk
Haleemah Aduke acquires the art of Quran as she learns to
     walk.
Omo Baba, aduke opo manlewa majaalekan, Superstar, the
     first of her words
Our superstar encapsulating all the stars in the sky!
The name given to a child comes true for the child
The name of the lioness has come true for my baby
Crushing all contenders to emerge the ruler of the sky
Superstar, "I'm a Superstar!" has proven true of my daughter,
Onikepe Aduke Opo!

Section 2

Baban Gani Eto!

If you have seen him before
You can never miss him again, day or night
The sonorous voice of Baban Gani Eto
The uniqueness of his Ilorin mark, the Facial Mark of the
    City of Light
Baban Gani with texture in his voice—only an Ilorin born
    boasts such a juicy voice
Baba Gani in Omoda, in Alore, Baban Gani in Abemi, In
    Pakata, Itakudinma,
Baba Gani in Ita Ogunbo, In Alanamu, In Adifa, Oja Oba,
    Gambari
Baba Gani all over,
Ilorin, over and over again, the Poet of Waka, The solo Waka
    of Fame
Baba Gani in light and darkness, chanting and drumming all
    by mouth!
You would dance without knowing you are dancing
You would smile without knowing you are smiling
You would be drawn into the humour of a legendary
    performer
The solo performer of Ilorin Waka
You would be drawn into the humor and the art, art of the
    humorous at their peak
Baba Gani attains the peak with every performance
He knows the peak of every Ilorin
And attains it over and over again for Ilorin
Baba Gani Eto!

Shehu Salihu Baba Oba

When some people dream, they dream of crowns and royal
robes
They dream of palaces and royal convoys
Yet one person's dream is the greatness of Ilorin
His dream is about how he meets his Lord and asks that this
city stand for him as evidence of his *ibadah* to God
Shehu Salihu's dream is to attract saints of God to his city
To root knowledge of Allah in a town with no equal
His dream was a dream of Quranic voices, a dream of ethnic
flavours all in the service of Ilorin
His dream was a dream of Ilorin where knowledge gives
birth to actions
And actions, according to piety
Salihu's dreams is for his children to accept leadership of the
Emirate
To rule with truth to ancestry, and to fortify ancestry's
history of fairness and Godliness
His dreams are for love: love of self, love of town, and love of
God
He dreams of Ilorin children, passionate in love for each
other!
He left signs for all to know his dreams are the robes of Ilorin
culture
"Robe on," he says to Ilorin
Shehu Salihu says, "Robe on," to Ilorin
Alfa Alimi says, "Robe on," to all and assume the dignity and
honour
Which only truth can bestow!

AbdulKadir Orire

Who says a name doesn't denote destiny!
I have been witness to names that explain exactly the destiny
    of our Sarkin Malamai
The Ilorin's Sarkin Malamai, first among equals of elephants
    in our forest.
His head, through name, has been a head-for-good-fortune,
    Orire!
From Sokoto, a good-fortune for giving names to many,
    Asomo dolori ire, turning many young names to heads of
    good-fortune!
First named, first head of Sharia, holding forth for fairness
    and justice!
Like Emir AbdulKadir, this is Orire of justice and fairplay
Symbol of Ilorin piety known to all lions of the North
AbdulKadir Orire is the Zaki of Sharia, pathfinder of Islamic
    powers of the masses
Then, Secretary General, Jamaatu Nasrul Islam
Another trait of good-fortune for the Muslims, the pious as
    Bábá Akòwe of Jamaatu!
Khadi Secretary, Practical First in the banners of history!
Also, Sarkin Malamai, the first among giants of scholarship,
    King of Teachers!
Malamai uban dalibai, teachers superior to *talibs*!
Your fountains are springs for drinking!
Another first in the house of Ilorin
AbdulKadir Orire, you are the house of good fortunes!
You are a sun whose rays spread good fortune to the universe
    of Ilorin

Your light has illuminated this city, and shared its image
among the Muslims of Kwara, the *ummah* of Muhammed
across Nigeria!

Ibrahim Sulu Gambari, Emir of Dignity

Ilorin had emirs, AbdulSalam to AbdulKadir Baba-agba,
Never before the Emir, notorious for sharp justice even
   before the throne
Ibrahim's eagerness was from the bench of Justice
Eagerness to give justice evident of his ancestry!
Ibrahim, eagerness for economic buoyance:
Ilorin must lead in industry and commerce!
Ibrahim's Ilorin must chase poverty away to the trench!
No Justice with poverty, Emir Ibrahim Sulu's adage
Ilorin, house and village, must breed in abundance.
Ibrahim Sulu Gambari, the love of ancestor is the wisdom of
   the erudite
Ibrahim creates a wealth of words, wealth of thoughts,
   wealth of materials
Ilorin of Ibrahim Sulu booms in wealth from all angles of the
   sphere
Wealth of palace, wealth of children who are leaders all over
Wealth of scholars, who understand the actual names of God,
And invoke their meanings on behalf of their City
They recite in voices only Ilorin is bestowed.
Wealth of the palace grows in bounty of beauty
Wealth of a Central Mosque that is a wonder for guests and
   natives
Wealth of clothes many esteeming the the majesty of our
   Emir
Ibrahim's Ilorin must chase poverty away to the trenches!
No Justice with poverty, Emir Ibrahim Sulu's adage.
Our Emir looks askance unto Him, the Lord of the Worlds:

Wealth for my people from all it manifests!
Dignity for me, dignity for my people
Ibrahim Sulu Gambari, Emir of Dignity.

Kayo-Kayo

It's all about food, eat here and there and eat more!
Children love food; Ilorin children have a festival of food,
Festival of eating food, *kayo-kayo*, to be stomach-filled, to
    eat and be stomach full
Such varieties of food!
I've never before seen a festival of eating to fill you so much,
    except in Ilorin
Children's festival of *Kayo-Kayo*, eating to fill, and eating to
    sing
Goat and Lamb meat from Ramadan, kept to dry in the roof,
Yam and yam flour, special flavours of cooking
Varieties of Ilorin *tuwo* and *amala*, all to the draw of *ila* and
    luru soup
And to the delicious royalty of the dried meat
Kayo-Kayo is the children's lore of songs and food,
Festival of branching at compounds and houses
Of knocking on the doors with Ilorin songs of food
Festival of the children's molars dancing,
At the thrill of our mothers' pots of soup
Kayo-Kayo of *oka-amala*, *kayo-kayo* of *ora-ama*, *kayo-
    kayo* of *eegun*, *kayo-kayo* of *iyan-ewu*
And of *oka-idagbona*, festival of eating and drinking, festival
    of children!
Kayo-Kayo, the festival of eating to full, festival of Ilorin!

The First Makama of Ilorin

Allah's destiny, love of town in the marrows of bone.
Alhaji Oniye, the love of Ilorin is the beginning of wisdom!
From time, a labour of love for the city of wisdom, the city of
    knowledge
All Ilorin is home to our Fathers
Whoever is not known to Oniye is not born of Ilorin!
All areas of the town are areas of Oniye,
Comb the city for service of culture, service of love
Oniye serves Ilorin: culture, safety, religion, always for
    number one!
Alhaji Oniye, *Alaali* of Ilorin!

Makama from birth!
Whether asleep or awake, Oniye's mouth swings like a lion
His voice is the voice of destiny,
He's never spoken without hearing laughter in return
All speeches of Oniye are honey in the ears of Ilorin
Oniye speaks,
And receives smiles of love, smiles of gratitude.

Makama from birth,
Whether asleep or awake, Oniye's mouth swings like a lion
Ilorin's heart of speechmaking is the heart of Oniye
He gives his speech the flavor only Ilorin can give
Ibrahim Oniye, Ilorin's tongue of salt
The first Makama of Ilorin, Ibrahim Oniye is number one!
Ilorin Emirate is number one!
for Oniye, Ilorin is number one!

Sherifu-deen of Ilorin

Sherifu-Deen, the horse of wisdom!
The horse of Ilorin, the horse of Islam!
If you don't know what the horse is made of, speak to
    Sherifu-deen,
His guard is the guard of the Ilorin horse
His Guard is the Guard of the City, the protector of Faith
The Sherif of Islam, nothing must threaten the city of God
There is no place without God, but He dwells in Ilorin!
I've seen Sherif jump to the sky just to clear a cloud he saw
    dirtying his city
I've seen him enter rocket clothes, and spoken fiery fires as if
    the world would crack
When you ask to fight for food, don't call sherif,
Fight for money, don't ask sherif
Contest for clothes, sheriff won't answer your call.
Guard of the City, Guard of Ilorin
Endeavours for Islam, you need not call,
Sherif has already sniffed your mind and responded with his
    being!
His body waters boil when strangers deface our city
His eyes' liquid gets hotter, whenever anyone pours filth on
    Faith
He's gone to battle, not because he's in the military
But because Ilorin is in him,
It is in his blood to defend its sovereignty, the Islamic
    sovereignty of Ilorin!
Sherifu-deen of Ilorin! *Magaji* of Ile Olowo, *Isale* Gambari!

Oniwasi Agbaye, Aminullahi!

Ya Rabbi, da baba lola, fiwon si aljanna onidera!
Ya Rabbi, da baba lola, fiwon si qiyama onidera!
Alahumma Amin, Alahuma Amin, ya Allah, da baba lola!

Preacher of faith, preacher of Islam,
Lion of Islam, The Preacher of the World!
If haven't seen Oniwasi Agbaye in his act, you've never seen a
   preacher indeed!
Oniwasi Agbaye, pupil of Kamaluddeen, has no words
   outside his teacher's!
He nails every speech with a quote from his teacher:
His eyes brightening like sudden sunshine lights up a
   darkling day, *Nigbati Alhaji Agba...! Nigbati Alhaji*
   Agba...!
He quotes his teacher as if he's back in school again, as if he's
   right in front of him.
Oniwasi Agbaye, he's fulfilled when his teacher's thoughts
   rekindle his mind.

Ya Rabbi, da baba lola, fiwon si aljanna onidera!
Ya Rabbi, da baba lola, fiwon si qiyama onidera!
Alahumma Amin, Alahuma Amin, ya Allah, da baba lola!

Preacher of faith, preacher of Islam,
Lion of Islam, the Preacher of the world!
Aminullahi of Abata, Alhaji Abata, *Kamaliyya* to his
   students and mates.

He is the *Adabiyyatul Alkamaliyya*, the core *Al-Adab*, of
    Kamaliyya!
Oniwasi Agbaye, preserving memory for classmates,
Preserving nobility for students, born and unborn!
Aminullahi forges a path, mindful of the pride of his
    colleagues!
Asking apprentices to follow the way of *Kamaliyya, al-
adabiyyatu al-kamaliyyatu!*

Ya Rabbi, da baba lola, fiwon si aljanna onidera!
Ya Rabbi, da baba lola, fiwon si qiyama onidera!
Alahumma Amin, Alahuma Amin, ya Allah, da baba lola!

Preacher of faith, preacher of Islam
Lion of Islam, the Preacher of the world!
When the hen hatches, she covers her brood with her
    feathers
Giving them warmth, protecting them from havoc
The lion and the lioness, their eyes keep danger away from
    their cubs,
Mother lion breastfeeds day and night, ensuring her children
    taste no hunger!
Aminullahi, abiyamo toto, the-father-who-gives-birth and
    never again goes to sleep
Oniwasi Agbaye never slept, constantly seeking peace and
    security for us,
Your *Abiyamo* never heard your children's cries and cringed!

Ya Rabbi, da baba lola, fiwon si aljanna onidera!
Ya Rabbi, da baba lola, fiwon si qiyama onidera!
Alahumma Amin, Alahuma Amin, ya Allah, da baba lola!

Preacher of faith, preacher of Islam
Lion of the Qur'an, Preacher of the world
One day at the Emir's palace, all sit in festivity
Festival of Quran, Contest of Voices,
Ilorin's recitation in voices
Oba Ilorin and his subjects toast the day to the eve of *Eid*
Aminullahi, preacher of piety,
Mounting the porch isn't a problem, speaking with piety is
    like eating a banana for our father!

Ya Rabbi, da baba lola, fiwon si aljanna onidera!
Ya Rabbi, da baba lola, fiwon si qiyama onidera!
Alahumma Amin, Alahuma Amin, ya Allah, da baba lola!

He uses words even a deaf ruler's ears would hear
He swears he is Man enough to carry all consequences
If it's the words of Quran!
Oniwasi Agbaye's trepidations are the sanctity of Quran
Sanctity of the City that loves God without ceasing
He preaches to power and preaches to the powerless
Those who take lightly a premonition of an *Adabiy*
Aminullahi proves for them the blistering of the sun in the
    house of *Adabiyya*!
That it provides light and brightness doesn't mean the sun
    won't burn those who fail
To caution their callous indulgences!

Ya Rabbi, da baba lola, fiwon si aljanna onidera!
Ya Rabbi, da baba lola, fiwon si qiyama onidera!
Alahumma Amin, Alahuma Amin, ya Allah, da baba lola!
Preacher of faith, preacher of Islam

Lion of the Qur'an, Preacher of the world
You've left your children in the hands of time!
Your *Abiyamo* never heard your children's cries and cringed!
Ilorin needs your prayers even more than before!

Ya Rabbi, da baba lola, fiwon si aljanna onidera!
Ya Rabbi, da baba lola, fiwon si qiyama onidera!
Alahumma Amin, Alahuma Amin, ya Allah, da baba lola!

Section 3

En so nilorin o eheee!

Enso nilorin o eheee
Enso nilorin o haa
Ilorin Afonja erinso nilorin
Ilorin Afonja erinso nilorin

Eni to fe merin ninun igbo
Eni to ba fe mefon lodan
Eni tio mun ogongo oba ninu odo
Yo patu t'amu erin mpa
Yo dara tamefon nda ninu igbo
Yo dangajia ninu apeja lodo!

Enso nilorin o eheee
Enso nilorin o haa
Ilorin Afonja erinso nilorin
Ilorin Afonja erinso nilorin

Eni ti yo ma asiri onile koya fara monile
Eni tofe masiri oloko koya yo moloko
Eni to fe ma ibi t'olodo tin saragidi, ko ya feju re sile bi ósùn
Eni toba fe mase Ilorin kowa bawa tankara tira lojude oba wa

Enso nilorin o eheee
Enso nilorin o haa
Ilorin Afonja erinso nilorin
Ilorin Afonja erinso nilorin

Awa kuku ni, awa na lan j'afonja nile Are Ilorin
Awan lan je baruba nile aboju meji
Awa na kuku lanje Omo tapa niso eja

Awa ni Omo Alfa Nda ni ifona Shiru
Awa ni, awa lomo Kemberi l'Awodi
Awa lomo Gambari loja gbooro

Enso nilorin o eheee
Enso nilorin o haa
Ilorin Afonja erinso nilorin
Ilorin Afonja erinso nilorin

Awa ni, awa lomo Fulani ni ga Afa
Awa lomo onifura da nono loja Oba
Awa lomo Iya elekoogbona oni kangu
Awa lanseda kulikuli ta tunfi robo muko
Tanje dodonkuwa alata feere
Awa lomo iya tuwo ni ile eleja
Tanfi warankasi sobe
Ti oka idagbona nlo tinrin tinrin lona ofun!

Enso nilorin o eheee
Enso nilorin o haa
Ilorin Afonja erinso nilorin
Ilorin Afonja erinso nilorin

Oni Lawani Lobawa, aafa lobawa ni Ilorin
Awani arikewu sola afi wala tore
Elenu mefa won a seko
Awon elenu mefa won a se'badan
Beeyan o lenu mejidilogun,
Koleselorin tiwa!

Enso nilorin o eheee
Enso nilorin o haa
Ilorin Afonja erinso nilorin
Ilorin Afonja erinso nilorin

Khalifatu Adabiyya, Alabi Ese!

Omo won nile Araagbaji, afikewu sola, afi tira dara, afi ima se
   faari
Alabi ese
Omo ese tinseni
Omo egba tingbarareele

Tala'ali Badiru alayna
Min thaniyyatil wada'i
Wajabash-shukuru alayna
Ma da'aa lillahi da'i

Won ni omo njo bábá, tie yi karama
Ojo Shaikh Kamaru to, atirin, atiwa, ateyinju, ti baba re
   kukuni
Arole Adabiyy, Omo Iya Ololele
Asabi mi owon, omo Balogun l'Ajikobi
Eni tobaferija Khalifa, koma kì iya Ololele leemeta
Emi kì won o, mokiyami, Asabi lemefa, motun so 'mo loruko
Asabi Opo, Malewa Majaalekan
Asabi nile Ajikobi, wa d'asabi Ile Ago, o d'asabi nile Akaje,
   Ajikobi kanna saani!

Tala'ali Badiru alayna
Min thaniyyatil wada'i
Wajabash-shukuru alayna
Ma da'aa lillahi da'i

Khalifat Adabiyya Ahmad Olayiwola
Eni toba fe waja Khalifa, kowemu ma defila
Yowa so eni tofijo
Tabi kofi suna re s'apo, ko ma dahun alaje
Yowa so eni tofijo nilorin
Nile llorin, ile aji tankara Kurani, Suna lawanje, koda taaba fi
    alaje ha laarin
Ilorin ke fun alaje niyi kowa bo suna male, afomale Ilorin!
Ahmad Olayiwola Kamal, omo to yayi nile Araagbaji, Ile
    Ilorin!

Tala'ali Badiru alayna
Min thaniyyatil wada'i
Wajabash-shukuru alayna
Ma da'aa lillahi da'i

Olooto aye, Olooto koda boba dorun,
Be fun omo Kamaru legberun owo, teba ti yo ooto sile,
Kini yo fowoyinse!
Ke m'aso olá toto wo lawujo, ti o basi ododo nibe, kia ni yo da
    asohun nun!
Anwa owolo apade iyi lona!
Baba Ahmad Folorunsho, Baba Ayanfe mi Ramatallahi
    Karamatudeen
Baba Muhammed Adeniyi Omo Iya Niyi
Ile kun, ita kun, albarika ninjebe!

Tala'ali Badiru alayna
Min thaniyyatil wada'i
Wajabash-shukuru alayna
Ma da'aa lillahi da'i

Nda Salati

How many people know why God's blessings increase in Ilorin
    day after day
It is because of the work done by Salati, Alfa Salati, Nda Salati,
    who used every breath to ask for blessings for Ilorin
Nda Salati— hardly any one compares to his *zikr* for *daraja*
    Ilorin
Nda Salati had a corner where he alone sat in prayer for his
    town
He's known as the Shehu, he who created fellowship and
    followers
Nda Salati, *Kadiriy wirdi*, the essence of devotion to the call of
    the Creator
None more than Salati in degree of devotion to His cause
Whatever he knew to be Allah's love, he used to beseech God for
    favours on Ilorin
Not for him, but for this town to be second to none
Nda Salati, Ilorin's symbol in devotion to God
Whatever you heard of Nda Salati, it is small compared to what
    the doyen had done in secret for Allah's mercies on his town
It is not for him that all whose hands have touched, and eyes
    have seen, and mouths have uttered, that all should know
God, the all knowing even before conception, already has
    known, and to Salati knowledge is what matters
The uncountable wonders of selfless devotion are hallmarks of
    our hero!
The hero of devotion, hero of sacrifice for the greatness of his
    city
Nda Salati, the spiritual hero of Ilorin!

Alfa Belgore

Alkalin Alkalai, Judge of Judges, colourful on the Bench of
    Nigeria!
When he became the Chief Justice at the Nation's Capital, the
    first from Ilorin
'Was as if None before had mounted the peak of Judiciary:
None before had such colours or was called Judge of a Nation!
Alfa's time was like "all-ever-spent" of Chief Justices since its
    creation
He got to business and mobilized for justice
Alfa proved his name,
He proved his ancestry, the Belgores of Ilorin:
Justice is the blood of the chaste!
They are the vessels of law of Ilorin
The vessels of Justice in the City of Knowledge
Belgore is the Alfa of Justice
Alfa, our Justice, son of an Ilorin Judge,
Son of a Judge of Arewa,
Father of Justices in Nigeria!

Ibrahim, the Lion of Love

How many lions do we see in the forest smiling at and cuddling
    with the other animals?
How many leopards touch the stomachs of giraffes only to
    sense how they are feeling?
How many in the house of *Serpent* spread their tails for young
    and old to walk over?
In the house of Ilorin, our Lion is a lion of love, our Tiger, a
    tiger of joy.
Our Serpent, a serpent of patience!
Ibrahim Sulu preaches love for young and elderly,
Our Philosopher Emir defines Love for children of Ilorin:
Love yourself, he says, and you will love others!
Every day when Ibrahim recites his love verses to Ilorin: *Eferan
    arayin, Olohun je kaferan ara wa*!
Ibrahim's *aaya* is for an Ilorin man to love himself,
And for an Ilorin woman to love herself,
Then all will love the other! And act towards each other with a
    heart of love!
Ibrahim Sulu Gambari, our Lion of Love
Your very eyes, our Emir of Affection, would see your love
    prayers,
Meet Allah's choicest blessings for a City of Love!

Kosibi Tolohun o si, ama Ilorin ninsun

Orin Odolaye Aremu, Alalaye Ilorin ni:
Oni, Kosibi t'Olohun o si, ama Ilorin ninsun
Oni, N sule Gambari Alaafin Ilorin!

Ile Ilorin Ile Olohun ni, Ile Ilorin Ile Olohun
Oko Ilorin, Oko Olohun ni, omi Ilorin Omi Olohun
Allahu Rabi tio fi Ilorin sile nigba kan!

Orin Odolaye Aremu, Alalaye Ilorin ni:
Oni, Kosibi t'Olohun o si, ama Ilorin ninsun
Oni, N sule Gambari Alaafin Ilorin!

Ilorin Afonja enu dun iyo te,
Ilu tobi toyi o leegun rara
Esin legun ile won oko loro ibe:
Afonja de kaya, Afonja de loko
Afonja de Lailaha Ilallahu!

Orin Odolaye Aremu, Alalaye Ilorin ni:
Oni, Kosibi t'Olohun o si, ama Ilorin ninsun
Oni, N sule Gambari Alaafin Ilorin!

Omo arikewu sola
Omo afi walaa tore
Igi Ilorin, afa ni,
Ewure Ilorin, afa ni
Igunta Ilorin, afa,

Ambele omolorin, omoluabi, omokewu!
Latikekere nimale tinkoma re nikewu,
Ilorin, Afa baba Oba!

Orin Odolaye Aremu, Alalaye Ilorin ni:
Oni, Kosibi t'Olohun o si, ama Ilorin ninsun
Oni, N sule Gambari Alaafin Ilorin!

Sheu Alimi, Babanla wa, afa ni
Sheu AbdulSalam, Oba ni, omo afa ni
Shehu
Ase Afa ni Baba Oba nilorin!

Orin Odolaye Aremu, Alalaye Ilorin ni:
Oni, Kosibi t'Olohun o si, ama Ilorin ninsun
Oni, N sule Gambari Alaafin Ilorin!

Eni toba koyan Ilorin kere,
Ohun ni o ni ronje ninu abo
Koda koni riyo ninu obe
Odolaye ni, Ilorin o loko, ko lodo
Asinje ntowuwa nigba gbogbo!

Orin Odolaye Aremu, Alalaye Ilorin ni:
Oni, Kosibi t'Olohun o si, ama Ilorin ninsun
Oni, N sule Gambari Alaafin Ilorin!

Ife Ilorin t'Olohun fe
Lanfi nse faari ni gba gbogbo
Ohun Ilorin to fise faari: Kurani, Oba wa, Ifaya bale, Afa Ilorin,
Olowo Ilorin,

Omo kekere Ilorin, agbagba Ilorin Obinrin Ilorin, Okunrin
Ilorin, gbogbo lorin lapapo!
Eni t'Olohun fe kose farawe,
Ilu toba fara welorin yo kan'buku!

Orin Odolaye Aremu, Alalaye Ilorin ni:
Oni, Kosibi t'Olohun o si, ama Ilorin ninsun
Oni, N sule Gambari Alaafin Ilorin!

Ilorin Ete!

Jaigbade Alao, Oba Olorin
Oni Ilorin Ete ni,
Oni, Ogbon lopo nilorin toju ti gbogbo won lo!

Ti'lorin ba lo soju ogun, Ilorin aje ogun
Ilorin amu ere ogun wale,
Niwaju lehin, Ilorin akowon je!

Jaigbade Alao, Oba Olorin
Oni Ilorin Ete ni,
Oni, Ogbon lopo nilorin toju ti gbogbo won lo!

Be ba ri omo Ilorin tinbo, keya teri ba,
To ri Omo Ilorin, lolohun ni koni Ogbon ati ete ti won fin
*   jagun*
Ilorin Ete ni!

Jaigbade Alao, Oba Olorin
Oni Ilorin Ete ni,
Oni, Ogbon lopo nilorin toju ti gbogbo won lo!

Eleran, elelubo, alaso,
Teeba doja Ibadan, abed'oja Eko
Won o le kooyin je
Olohun Oba lofogbon Oja dayin lola
Olohun Oba lofoye ati ima dayin lola!

Jaigbade Alao, Oba Olorin
Oni Ilorin Ete ni,
Oni, Ogbon lopo nilorin toju ti gbogbo won lo!

Bilorin bantaja n rere je
Bilorin ban raja n rere je
Bilorin ba r'ogun nrere je
Bo lorin ban jogun nrere je
Wan jowu Ilorin, won jowu Olohun!

Jaigbade Alao, Oba Olorin
Oni Ilorin Ete ni,
Oni, Ogbon lopo nilorin toju ti gbogbo won lo!

Won o ma pe ise Olohun ni
Aduha Babanla Ilorin logba tobe
Aduha Shehu Alimi Baba Oba
Aduha Afonja Omo Laderin

Jaigbade Alao, Oba Olorin
Oni Ilorin Ete ni,
Oni, Ogbon lopo nilorin toju ti gbogbo won lo!

Awa wi talai wi, woni Ilorin Mesu Jamba!
Jamba bawo, Omo Adama?!
Eni tio toni tin dena deni,
Kori ohun wi ma, on kigbe Jamba kakiri
Ilorin Ete ni, Kise Jamba rara!

Jaigbade Alao, Oba Olorin
Oni Ilorin Ete ni,
Oni, Ogbon lopo nilorin toju ti gbogbo won lo!

Ogbon nio, Olohun lofun wa logbon
Gbigba aduha ni, Olohun ningbaduha
Alubarika ni, tolohun fun lorin
Kese Jamba rara!

Jaigbade Alao, Oba Olorin
Oni Ilorin Ete ni,
Oni, Ogbon lopo nilorin toju ti gbogbo won lo!

Te batun gbo tiwon wi pe Mesu Jamba,
Ke ranwon leti Orin Jaigbade Alao, Oba Olorin
Ilorin, Ete ni
Ogbon lopo nilorin to ju ti gbogbo won lo!
Ilorin Ete ni!

Jaigbade Alao, Oba Olorin
Oni Ilorin Ete ni,
Oni, Ogbon lopo nilorin toju ti gbogbo won lo!

Ti won ba fe ko ogbon kiwon o wi
Ti won ba fe ko ima kiwon o so
Kiwon o gbafun Oba Yarabi toti dajo
To ti ko are funlorin,
To ni Kurani ni yoma bori
Olohun nio,
Oni Ilorin ni yo ma jeja
Yoma jeja won lo layelaye
Ilorin Ete!

Jaigbade Alao, Oba Olorin
Oni Ilorin Ete ni,
Oni, Ogbon lopo nilorin toju ti gbogbo won lo!

Section 4

Saka Nuru

Ilorin ranks firsts, all around, Ilorin First Eagles in the nest
of Birds!
First Chief Justice, Appeal Court President, First Professor,
First Lawyer, and First!
Saka Nuru is the First among Professors hailing from Ilorin!
He combed Zaria like no person has ever combed a city
He is the Diamond that gives birth to other diamonds,
Ilorin's Diamonds have a king, Saka Nuru is it!
He has conquered all he sets his hands on and brings it back
home:
Treasures only the greatest diamond could possess!
Saka went to white man's land and got the spoils from
abroad
He went to Zaria and brought back the spoils of Zazzau!
He brought them home and the spoils are booties of pride to
Ilorinland!
Long before any Ilorin became a teacher in a Citadel, Saka
Nuru earned leadership among the eggheads of Zaria
He was called to the Bar of knowledge and served with
passion and decency
Saka, a learned principal who led troops of learned birds
He performed this feat many times over and became the
darling among the academic lords!
Ask Zaria for their stories and they would paint the world
with them!
If you are a lord in academia, Saka Nuru has been there
before!
Our Iroko tree, his branch arms see far into the forest

In his hands, no birds fear to fly!

Agboola Gambari, Diplomat of the World!

The people of Ilorin count their blessings
And say *alhamdulillahi* daily for the mercies of God!
Agboola, royalty has no limit, spreading out like an ocean
 that sprawls without ending!
The *lekeleke* bird spreads wings of peace, wherever he flies
 his wings cast a calming cover
The *lekeleke* bird is the bird we sing for. We beckon, bring
 your peace here:
Lekeleke bunmi loka, mu dudu lo mu funfun bowale!
Bird of peace, give me your ring, take away our sorrow, and
 bring home your peace!
The African *lekeleke* is the cynosure of the world,
Spreading its wings and giving its rings!
From Rwanda to Myanmar to Darfur
This Ilorin son is the planter of the seed
Germinating across the world!
Diplomat of the World
The Royal of Ilorin, lineage of Alimi
You gave the whole world an image of your birth
You represented Alfa Alimi to the world in disarray and
brought them peace
You proved to the world that the royalty of our town
Is the royalty of knowledge, is the royalty of scholars,
The royalty of peace!

Omo Ilorin

Ewa bami korin f'omo Ilorin
Omo Alimi Omo Afonja
Omo Kembari, Omo Gambari
Omo Tapa, Omo Baruba
Gani yafiji Omo alalubarika!
Ilorin lobi omo iyi omo aponle
Samanri nunni, Gbogbo ibi to yosi, omo ti wan fin toro omo
     ni
Omoluabi, Omokewu, Omo tin tankara kurani nigba
     gbogbo
Omo ti wanfin toro Omo, Ilorin sa lolohun bun!

Omo tin ye omode si, asi ye agba si
Omo lorin ni omo tin ri baba re feekun mejeji lele
Omo tin ri iya re tin yika otun tin yika osi
Aso wipe, mama mi aduha yin naa ni
Omo ti wanfin toro Omo, Ilorin sa lolohun bun.

Omo toma iyi Oba to ma iyi ijoye
Omo tin tiju magaji ile omo ti tiju Imamu ladugbo
Omo tinse iyi fun Alfa nile kewu, omo tinse iyi tisa ni ile iwe
Omo gidi, omo itiju.

Omo to r'oba to pon Oba wa le,
To ma seeeuu pe, to sin ye Oba Ilorin si, to si ntun saduha
     fun oba wa:
Tin ban tin se samasangudu f'arole Alimi,
Nin tun sope, Wallahu Ya'asimuka Mina Nasi f'oba.

Gbogbo Oloye oba to bari, aduha nin ma nfi ranse s'oba wa
   nilorin
Seeeuuu, Seeeuuu, nin fi ranse s'oba, koda bi esin oba wa
   lori tinkojalo
Benle kori awon Balogun Ilorin wa
Paapa, kori Magaji Aare, abi Babab Isale,
Bori Imamu Agba abi Imamu Imale, abi Imamu Gambari,
Seeeuu nio ma pe seeeuu ranse lenu Omo Ilorin

Omo itiju oma alaubarika tinwuyan
Atokunrin, atobinrin, nilorin finse faari,
B'oma Ilorin bari iyamin tinlo, b'oma Ilorin bari baba mi
   tinbo wa,
Orin aduha na l'omo Ilorin nfi senu,
Aani, Eni sagbako b'olohun fe
Ani, Oju aye koni tiyin, boba wola Muhamma mi, Omo
   alalubarika nio bun yin,
Koni bunyin ni gbemi gbemi!
Omo Ilorin Omo aduha,
Omo giriki Omo Koreyi, aduha baba gba!

Omo Ilorin, Omu Iya dun!
Ti omo Ilorin ba ko sagbada ti won se kayan sama si,
To ba wo buba le sanyan, to ro ipele
Abi ole ntelaafa lowo lewu tin se faaji kakiri Ilorin,
Omo ni Omo fa, Omo iyi Omu iya dun!

Loya AbdulRazak, Omo Ukku Ukku!

Refrain: *Omo Ilorin tinje Rasaki, Loyan girki*
         Omo gidi omo ukku ukku!

Gbogbo Ilorin ni omo ukku ukku,
Koda ko je Baruba, koje Gobiri onjijo ukku ukku!
Loya akoko ni gbogbo Arewa, AbdulRazak loya tin pe loya
     ranse
Gbogbo ile re asan ofín ni, gbogbo koro yara asan iwe!
To bari AbdulRazak toge fila segbekan tinse faari Ilorin,
AbdulRazak tobe oju beelo, "taalo to kowa fagagbaga!" ni
     orin tinko lenu,
Boronkini loya, ta tie lo tobe gan tio f'aya ko loya
     AbdulRazak ti aya re o ni kè!

Omo Ilorin tinje Rasaki, Loyan girki
Omo gidi omo ukku ukku!

Ta lo tobe gan ti yo sarifin si omo Ilorin to dangajia ninu
ofin,
Omo to somo giriki ninu iwa,
Lati aye tindaye l'Abdulrazaq ti kundun Ilu re
Tose gudugudu meje tose yaya mefa
To ko ilewe kan, ara nla ni,
Ilorin College Ilorin, AbdulRazak ni agbada nla ti ko kii da
     obe nun!

Omo Ilorin tinje Rasaki, Loyan girki
Omo gidi omo ukku ukku!

Omo ekun sebi ekun ni yojo
Kasise taratara, kaferan ilu, kako ere ise se ebun bun ilu,
    sebi isé Baba ré ni
Awon tobi é lomo ase ilu bi enin se adini ni wonje!
Loya AbdulRazak ti awon ara ile re ndupe fun
Wipe koda boku kobo lapo, yo fi se ebi lore ni,
Bosi ku sisi abi ku sile kan, gba ni yo se fun ara adugbo!
Lofi fi owo taara ko Ile iwe jo, ti ilu sin se enma!

Omo Ilorin tinje Rasaki, Loyan girki
Omo gidi omo ukku ukku!

Ima lo je AbdulRazak logun, ofima ma ara Ilorin
Oye lo je logun, ofi oye ma ilu re
Iyi ataponle lo jee logun
Ofun ilu re niyi, ofun ilu re laponle
Seri bi gbogbo omo AbdulRazak tin niyi tin won laponle
Ise Owo baba won ni,
Otonkiri Loya tinje AbdulRazaki!

Omo Ilorin tinje Rasaki, Loyan girki
Omo gidi omo ukku ukku!

Ile ya, fara ile ewa re ile,
Ajo ya fara ajo ewa r'ajo,
Ukku ukku ya fara Ilorin, ewa korin ukku ukku fajape
Loya Abdulrazak!

Omo Ilorin tinje Rasaki, Loyan girki
Omo gidi omo ukku ukku!

Wazirin Geri, the test of a patriot!

We have seen elephants in the forests, never have they been
   as mighty as this elephant!
We have seen lions and leopards, never have we seen the
   gorgeousness of this one!
Whoever boasts to know giraffe hasn't seen a hippopotamus!
Wazinrin Gerin Ilorin, never before a greater colossus
   descended from our city of joy!
Olooye, Agoro fed Ilorin towns and villages and asked all
   Kwarans to take their forage!

Who sees the Atlantic Ocean or the Pacific Ocean go dry?
Olooye, it is wealth bearing a borrowed name that goes to dry,
The wealth of your sweat has proven greater than an ocean in
   the land of Ilorin
Omo alaali Ilorin, a true born that makes his city of joy an
   everlasting joy!
How can one have this son as her child and not be
   overwhelmed with joy!
Ask our Emir his joyful song and gratitude to God
Ask Ilorin downtrodden how they prayed that Allah will
   forever keep Saraki beyond his dreams!

The tests of patriots are tests of bravery!
In the middle of War, patriots choose with valor,
Not one chitchats away their home to maurauders!
Oloye stood his ground to military and civilian maurauders,

Who tried to castigate the nobility of his ancestral Ilorin.
Olooye has always chosen to uphold the diginity of his
    ancetral home
Saraki offered his life and the life of his offspring to protect
    his land!

Whoever wants to belittle Saraki has our Emir to fight
Such a person has the masses to face, for as long as Ilorin has
the Quran, Ilorin can't be defeated!
Saraki turned politics into substance for his city of Ilorin:
A road network, water for drinking, and food of all kinds in
    house after house!
Politics of infrastructure, politics of food
Politics of education, politics of wealth
Olooye's politics are politics of joy!
Wazirin Geri, Olusola Saraki, it is God that brought this
    wealth
God brought this joy to the household of Ilorin.

If you say you are rich whatever your city, don't try to boast
    to Ilorin
Ilorin has seen the wealthy eating with the masses from one
    pot of soup!
With the footsteps Olooye printed on our sand, no wealthy
    would again bamboozle the City of Ilorin!

Pacesetters

Pacesetters are the dwellings of our City
Pacesetters in peace and harmony
Ilorin dwellings set the pace for other cities to follow
When it is time to choose from food of life
Ilorin chooses Quran—the food for the soul
Ilorin opts for the food of the mind
Knowing it grows healthy bodies grows peace
When it is time to choose the cloth of life
Ilorin dwellings choose the habit of harmony
Ilorin sets the pace in the City of Diversity,
As the City of Harmony!
To Ilorin, the City of Ethnicities,
Diversity is Harmony!
Come, Ilorin, come see this City!
Yoruba, Hausa, Fulani, Kamberu, Baruba, Nupe
All harmony is Islam, Islamicity of Harmony!
Pacesetters in the Harmony of Life!
This City has found its cause, no going back for Ilorin,
To create chaos, improbable!
Those who attempted told stories of self-destruction!
Yes, self-destroyers attempted chaos into the Harmony of
    Ilorin:
Pacesetter of Harmony in Diversity!

Bukola, the child for whom Oloye is praised!

Oloye Bábá Bukola, a child's name is praise for his father
Bukola, the child for whom Oloye is praised!
A father's love is permanent for his children; a mother's love
    for her children lasts an eternity!
Right from infancy, Oloye carried his child high on his
    shoulders,
Carried him to mount beside him on the horse to the Emir's
    Palace
Beside him, Abubakar sat holding the hooks in imitation of
    his father!
 Here, father and son taking their turn on the horses of the
    Ilorin festival
A town as big as this does not have Egungun
Horses are the Masquerades of Ilorin's household
Our horses are our rides to the mountains of power!
Whenever they look and see horses, they run away for fear of
falling
Who dares face Ilorin's horses eager to conquer!
When Ilorin people are on their horses no one is man enough
    to stand in their way
Kings and warriors fall as they yell: Ilorin is a colossus for
    our thoughtless bid!
Here they surrender to the mighty tactics,
Our Baloguns bring home the spoils of war,
Ilorin's stratagem they are unable to sort!

Ilorin's fathers have fortified their children with *fatiha
    alalubarika*
Little should wonder when Ilorin's child is soaring high
It is inherent in the immunity of father of son, of mother of
    daughter!
Their children shall be taller than them!
OmoIlorin hasn't risen yet; Bukola hasn't risen yet,
The sky is only a beginning!

The Corners of Ilorin

How many streets have you travelled in Ilorin,
When you claim to know the corners of our town?
How many corners have you touched,
When you infer your knowledge of the nooks and corners of
    Ilorin?
Corners with children's games, where Ilorin fields celebrate
    soccer stars
Corners where children compete in bicycle ridding and
Often show how they surpass each other playing table tennis
There are corners offering delicious *tuwo* or rice and beans
And corners of *masa*, *fura* and *nono*, where *kangu* and
    guguru and *epa* can exercise the mouth
Ilorin corners are corners where we celebrate the legends of
    Quranic schools
Where children learn to complement western knowledge by
    going to learn the Quran
Corners are bound in galas of songs, from *Iyamin tinlo* to
    Iyamin Loilo
Corners where every time during the Eid, we walk around
    visiting our relatives
Ilorin corners are full of life, for children and for adults,
Where generations meet, one learning from the other.
Everyone loves to touch Ilorin corners,
The adults seek to show they are fully in charge
And the young have the fun that goes with growing up
Ilorin corners are for rearing children
And nurturing them to be true to Ilorin
Areas of Ilorin are areas of culture

Corners of Ilorin are corners of tradition
Some evenings, preachers are pelting verbal pebbles on
    characters perturbing
Asking that all follow the Quran, the Book of Wisdom
And seek from Muhammed examples of ethics.
Ilorin children, active and learning.
Corners become corners of competition
Sonorous voices in song during the Ramadan
Ilorin children compete and learn to win or lose
All in fun llorin lives
Many other times, games of *boju-boju* or games seeking
    rocks on clay soil,
Whoever is winner gets his victory celebrated
In the joy that other kids regard him winner
And yes, winners among winners are children of Ilorin
Ilorin streets and corners of the twenty-first century,
Are empty of the plays that make Ilorin Garden of festivals
Eletronic streets of video games and televion shows
Replacing corners of competition and streets of festivals!
Ilorin of today, reclaim the streets of culture,
From these strange streets of violence from video games and
    TV shows!

Section 5

Aso-Ofi, clothes of all ages!

Clothes of the young, clothes of the elderly, clothes of the old
Aso-Ofi, the clothes of all ages!
Ilorin weaves the clothes for young and old
Aso-Ofi is the Ilorin cloth of folklore.
Only when the son of Ilorin becomes man enough does he
    wear the clothes of culture
Only when the daughter of Ilorin becomes woman enough
    does she wear the clothes of tradition
Clothes of father inherited by son and son's sons
Clothes of mother inherited by daughter and daughter's
    daughters
As new designs are made, the old Aso-Ofi gain reverence!
Aso-Ofi, clothes of Wolimat, clothes of marriage, clothes of
    naming
Clothes of life, enemy of death
Aso-Oke is an enemy when passing to the world beyond
Clothes of fertility for the son and the daughter
Focal point of the festivity of coming of age
Foe to all at the rituals of death!
Clothes of ages, clothes of seasons!
Once upon a time, Ilorin played host to a woman from
    Canada
And all she wanted was the clothes of life,
Anafi Aberi was quick to respond,
Alhaji Jawondo gave word
From every household an answer had come: Here, have our
    clothes of refinement!
Judges and lawyers, tycoons of all kinds, their roots from it!

The Canadian posed and turned around, all facets of human
    use,
Aso-Ofi on display for the world to see!
The clothes you wear, the wallet you hold, the shoe you use,
    the case for your eye glasses!
One who comes to Ilorin and asks not for Aso-Ofi
Had better not claim to have come to Ilorin
Aso-Ofi, Ilorin ancestral clothes of culture
Weaver of the cloths from the Loom of Ilorin!
Clothes of Aso-Ofi are clothes of wealth
Okuku, Kokogun, idasa, owu, ókò, siliki, idiofi are weaver's
    wealths!
The wealth of the young who go to school
Wealth of one man enough to hold a home
Wealth of the woman earning from the skills passed to her by
    her mother
Wealth of the tycoons on Market Days at Ibadan
Illustrious for his feats at home!
Industry of Ilorin is industry of clothes
Ilorin Industry is an industry of weaving!
Industry of the Loom and sewing and dyeing
And pressing, heavily heating rounds in sequence
Aso-Ofi is Ilorin's industry of design!

Warankasi

Refrain: *To ba j'omo Ilorin to ma waraje*
           Suegbe, suegbe lojeeee!
           Bojomo Ilorin Afonja toma waraje
           Suegbeee, suegbe lojeee!

Sagacious!
Delicious
Inviting!
Warankasi, inviting to the mouth of Ilorin

           To ba j'omo Ilorin to ma waraje
           Suegbe, suegbe lojeeee!
           Bojomo Ilorin Afonja toma waraje
           Suegbeee, suegbe lojeee!

Its wisdom, Warakasi's wisdom, is to enter without
     dissolving fast
It fills the mouth, overwhelming the tongue in sweetness
Warakansi's sweetness uniquely paramount to the tongues
     and molars
No one is able to discern before it spreads its coats!
It unfolds inside the mouth and the throat begins to beg to
     draw
Only a wise mouth responds to the throat's challenge, and
     refuses to yield without reaping its bounty

           To ba j'omo Ilorin to ma waraje

Suegbe, suegbe lojeeee!
Bojomo Ilorin Afonja toma waraje
Suegbeee, suegbe lojeee!

Warankasi, who knows how to praise thee until you visit with
    them?
Who understands what you mean until they feel your
    tenderness?
Who has the foresight to understand your flavour strictly
    from your aroma?
Even when they enter Garin Alimi, many palettes cannot
    detect your taste

To ba j'omo Ilorin to ma waraje
Suegbe, suegbe lojeeee!
Bojomo Ilorin Afonja toma waraje
Suegbeee, suegbe lojeee!

Try asking for Tuwo in Ilorin without knowledge to ask for
    Warakansi
Try asking the Iyamin Oloka to give you Oka without asking
    for Warankasi
Try speaking too much English saying cheese, not knowing
    the magic of Warankasi
Wasted, your visit's wasted! Even Ilorin hesitates to beckon
    for your return,
What value has the visit if the flavor of Warankasi makes no
    difference!

To ba j'omo Ilorin to ma waraje

Suegbe, suegbe lojeeee!
Bojomo Ilorin Afonja toma waraje
Suegbeee, suegbe lojeee!

Why the Sun has Not Diminished in Sunlight

Does he wonder why the sun has not diminished in sunlight?
Does he wonder why the sky has not turned red and the
  sands, yellow!
Ask him to wonder no more, because the sun's light is not
  sourced from his Generator Plant
He should wonder no more because they neither made from
  his ink the sky's colour nor from his ilk, the texture of the
  sands.
They wonder why Ilorin's fame hasn't dimished?!
Let them wonder! Wonder they wonder until they wonder
  wonder!
Ilorin's texture is not made of materials from their farms
If man has been the one giving the sun its strength,
Man would have ordered the sun to never shine on some
  regions of the earth!
Yet in the cold Antarctic, the sun has its day shining on the
  snow!
No matter what a child thinks of the taste of his mother's
  milk
It was the source of his survival as a baby.
Ilorin's sources of fame are not in their hands!
Not in the hands of their males and not in the hands of their
  females!
Those who question why Ilorin is so solid!
Question Ilorin and question God,
You questioned your birth, too!

Alfa Na'Allah

Ewa bami korin yi fun baba mi,
Alabi Opo, Manlewa Omo Saaratu Lakaje, Omo
    Muhammadu Golu!
Ahmad Na'Allah Bábá ni bábá
Baba atata, baba to ma giriki ni'wa!
Baba to ma pe, ima nikan na lole lani, ima Olohun ima
    alQuran ni o laayan!
Laaro ni, losan ni, tabele yanyan, kokuku sohun meji toju
    juu mima Olohun Oba lo
Kikewu, ti tankara Quanini lototo!
Baba yi ke to, wipe eyin omo min emalohun esi ye annabi si,
Epon Muhammdu le, kee tele oro asole tobatiso
Ke tele ona to file lele, ke ma sina
Babami ni, te ba kewu ke kawe, tori akewukewe laafin lo
    zamani gbadun!
Baba mi kuku ni, koburu wayi, te ba dara yin lokowo, ten
    pawoda soja
Tori, torokobo tenbanri yo senu lore, koni je ke tawona,
Kee se dandan ni kasise ijoba,
Won ni, koda besise ijoba ke mura ke dako to toko, ke
    dokowo manran
Iwalewa eyin omo de wonyi, Ahmad Na'Allah sope emo
    omo eni ti eyinse,
Ke ri ebi ke mun ebi lowo, ke ri ara ke fara mara, ke rajoji
    ke ki ajoji kaabo
Iwa rere dowo yin,
Won ni oruko rere, osunwon ju wura ohun fadaka lo

Olohun Oba Ya Rabbi, Oba Kanka, Dakun mojukoro ni laifi
  baba mi,
Ke kewon, Ke gewon, Ke fiwon salijanna
Bose pe ni tori ife ebi tiwon ni, ko dakun bawa fewon!
Boba je ti ife ti won fi han somo alaini, boku kobo ti won o lo,
  won o fi toro, dakun Olohun bawa kewon!
Boje ti kakoni ni kewu, ka koni ni Kurani, Kaso ibunsun dile
  eko, ka dajo kafi ti Olohun Oba dajo, dakun Olohun bawa
  kewon!
Ya Allahu Ya Rabbi, fiwon si aljannatu al-firdauz, kiwon o
  mule ti Annabi Muhammadu!

Bilikisu Esuu Oké

This is a song for my mother,
Bilikisu Esuu, daughter of Mohammadu Jimoh Mualubi in
    Ilorin
Daughter of Haleemah Asabi Iya Lele
Iya Lele who men faced and became dumbfounded
Unknowing how to tackle a woman that combines two
    strengths like the cobra
Iya Lele, slow to react against adversaries, but gargantuan in
    the punishment she renders!
If you didn't know Iya Lele you certainly have heard the
    name of Mama Olohuntoyin
Mother of "God is deserving of Praise"!
Iya Lele's daughter is patient to a fault, incapable of
    tolerating injustice
Whatever you ask of my mother, ask her not to lend you a
    hand to keep ants from finding their food!
Or causing them to go a mile longer than necessary to their
    feed.
She wouldn't discourage the eagles from flying as high as
    their feathers can take them
The humble Bilkisu will fight only to stop someone from
covering the Sunlight
Keeping our leaves from turning green
She would fight to keep the sky beautiful as a flower of night
And to allow children to learn from the blue sky what dance
it dances to attract the affection of the Sun!
My mother of love, my mother of caring,

Mother of Ilorin, Esuu Oké!